GARY SOTO

GARY SOTO
ONE KIND OF FAITH

CHRONICLE BOOKS
SAN FRANCISCO

Library of Congress Cataloging-in-Publication Data:
Soto, Gary.
One kind of faith / Gary Soto
p. cm.
ISBN 0-8118-4117-0
1. San Joaquin Valley (Calif.)–Poetry.   I. Title
PS3569.072054 2003
811'.54–dc21   2003004530

Manufactured in the United States of America

Book Design: Michael Osborne Design
Cover Illustration: José Ortega

Distributed in Canada by Raincoast Books
9050 Shaughnessy Street
Vancouver, British Columbia V6P 6E5

10 9 8 7 6 5 4 3 2 1

Chronicle Books LLC
85 Second Street
San Francisco, California 94105

www.chroniclebooks.com

Acknowledgments:
Some of these poems appeared in the following magazines: *Crazy Horse, Green Mountain Review, Indiana Review, Margie, Michigan Quarterly, Pedestal, Poetry, Quarterly West, Solo, The Threepenny Review,* and *TriQuarterly.* "Minimum Wage," "No Smoking, Please," "Self-Inquiry," "Street Scene on the Fulton Mall," "Dirt," and "Evening on the Lawn" appeared in *Poetry.* "Gil Mendez and the Metaphysics of a Blimp" appeared as a chapbook from Aureole Press in 2003.

THIS BOOK IS FOR DELOSS McGRAW

CONTENTS

PART ONE

The dogs look human in their Volvos,
Or so I discover as I walk through the parking lot of Longs Drugs,
Swinging my small purchase of antacids and vanilla ice cream.
All the dogs sit in their rightful places, the windows cracked.
Their mugs convey the look of, "No, I'm not what you think."
I call, "Hey, boy," to one pup who turns its head away, disgusted.
I call, "Hey, Lassie," to a golden retriever. To make her point,
She places her paws onto the steering wheel.
These dogs don't bark. Their eyes form words that say, "Go away."
I don't. When I look into the window of one car,
The dog busies itself checking the odometer for the next oil change.
How did this happen, this evolution in less than thirty years?
The pooches of my own childhood street fetched and frolicked,
Fought themselves into bloody rags. They copulated in a fury,
As we kids hollered, amazed by the pushpush action in the middle
Of the street. These Berkeley dogs practice their Zen
With the feng shui of water bowls set half-in, half-out of shadows.
These dogs know how to roll with Aikido.
They have lawyers, too, when divorce occurs
And resolution counselors when a fuss rises up between different breeds.
They know their rights.

The moon has no influence on these canines,
And the moon now rides high over the parking lot of Longs Drugs.
By this light I see a dog in every parked car reading the *Wall Street Journal*.
I'm still where I always was, a male dog with *Playboys* in the bottom drawer.
They have shifted from the backseat, to the passenger's seat,
To finally the driver's seat. When one set
Of owners returns from the store, they get into the back.
The dog gazes in the rearview mirror to see if its companions
Are buckled in, for they share in wills and deeds.
The Volvo starts with a shiver, leaves cautiously.
The companions smile at each other. They take up leashes
In their mouths, sniffing for the future.

The sound of nightfall was the chain
Looping around a pole and the click of a giant lock.
The security guard held up a girlie magazine
And slapped it against his knee,
His punishment for kicking his teacher in the head,
Thirty years before. Expelled, he drifted.
Now, duncelike, he sat on a stool,
A twenty-watt bulb shining on his face.
He was watching the raisin factory. Steam rose
From vents, and a single machine churned the raisins
For the nightshift. A forklift groaned,
A wrench for two men clanged against the cement.
His yawns could have raised a blimp.
O, Jesus, this man thought. If only a mule
Could appear and kick him in the head, hard for twenty years,
But now soft from inhaling the stink of washed raisins,
He looked at his magazine,
And the breasts were the color of raisins,
The eyes and hair, and down below
Raisins, too. A car passed and his eyes followed it,
The driver with the head of a raisin,
With little raisin children in the back,
One on his knees.

              The security guard shaded his eyes
From the light in his booth. But he couldn't keep
His hand up like that. The shame of it,
He saluting the first trucks
As they left the dock, loaded with raisins,
Lucky little bastards going somewhere sweet.

No one called but a cat,
This after I sat on the porch
And shot beetles with a rubber band.
Where were the jobs, hard ones or easy ones?
Last night I heard laughter on the television,
And I knew someone with his pants hitched
To his throat was paid to laugh—
A union job for crazies?
And me? This morning
I shot the slime
From beetles and studied my hands,
Soft as pears but bloody from the deaths
Of armored insects. My head lowered
To my chest. What was I but two eyeballs
Searching not my soul but the velvety fruits
Of kidney and spleen, the coiled intestine
Like the chain of a pocket watch.

The minutes poured through the hands of a neighbor's child.
This I saw from the porch, my landmark.
Now with the porch light bathing my head,
A cat called from a fence. And over that fence,
Between the wires feeding voices,
Angry as hornets, the moon was grinding through
Its gears as it pulled itself once more over pitched roofs.
What choice did I have? With no job,
I decided to steal from neighbors—
Bicycle, garden hose, rake with metal teeth
I could strike against the curb
And create fire.

The television
Was on and laughing at my scheme.
I followed the moon's milk spilled on asphalt.
In spite of my tramping, I returned home
With nothing but a dog I couldn't shake,
A single flea we shared—
He nibbling his paw like corn,
Me, unemployed writer, scratching my back
With the eraser of a chewed pencil.

Did you sneeze?
Yes, I rid myself of the imposter inside me.

Did you iron your shirt?
Yes, I used the steam of Mother's hate.

Did you wash your hands?
Yes, I learned my hygiene from a raccoon.

I prayed on my knees, and my knees answered with pain.
I gargled. I polished my shoes until I saw who I was.
I inflated my résumé by employing my middle name.

I walked to my interview, early,
The sun like a ring on an electric stove.
I patted my hair when I entered the wind of a revolving door.
The guard said, For you, it's the basement.

The economy was up. Flags whipped in every city plaza
In America. This I saw for myself as I rode the elevator,
Empty because everyone had a job but me.

Did you clean your ears?
Yes, not far from the drinking fountain's idiotic drivel.

Did you slice a banana in your daily oatmeal?
I added a pinch of salt, two raisins to sweeten my breath.

Did you remember your pen?
I remembered my fingers and my yawn as the elevator opened.

I shook hands that dripped like a dirty sea.
On the third day, I rose to the second floor.
I found a chair and desk. My name tag said my name.
Through the glass ceiling, I saw the heavy rumps of CEOs

Struggling to spell "tomorrow"—
One "r" or two. I sharpened my pencil
Into a wastebasket, kindling for a fire,
And pushed rigged contracts into the remarkable teeth
Of a hungry paper shredder.

Cigar smoke can't come into the famous-actor's house
And circle the mohair sofa not once but twice
And settle into the hair of the starlet crossing her legs,
The darkness about her knees worth the hour-long drive in traffic.
She twirls her wine glass and laughs. I claw
At the peanuts in a tray and wash my throat
With river run of cold beer. I go to the deck lit with Chinese lanterns,
Where a poodle wipes sludge from his eyes with a dirty paw,
His film role given to a beagle with a shiny coat.
Me, the dog, and the cigar. A screenwriter with no credits,
No one knows me. Thus, I drink.
Thus, I tickle my palm by raking it across a geranium,
My one pleasure. I breathe in
And out, red-tipped and glowing beneath my clothes.
By the end of the evening, what am I but ash. The wind
Of marketable legs crosses and recrosses, fanning me,
The dog, and, alas, the cigar with no lips to give the plot away.

The pile of autumn leaves smoked but didn't catch fire.
The rake lay with its teeth skyward.
A cat blinked. It was Saturday, near noon,
And I left that fire to follow a dog halfway up the block,
A stray with its back beaded with rain.
It had stormed somewhere, not on our street,
And the dog was wet. Geese were overhead,
And maybe Jehovah, too, with his own moist face,
Confused about the rising hemlines of once well-covered nuns.
I was thinking of the nuns myself, and thinking of such dogs,
Troubadours the color of smoke. I had told Sister Marie
That I wanted to be a saint, and if not a saint, then a dog.
She punished me with three quick snaps of her clicker . . .

But I'm here for the leaves. I'm here for the dog
That disappeared through a yard and exited through the alley.
In his own way, he provided a lesson. Leaves don't burn
When wet, and you must walk years for your answer:
This boy was not going to become a saint or dog
But a man, like any other, an employee with a sack lunch,
Someone flatfooted, someone between earth and sky.

My body lived briefly in the pupils of a dog,
One day friendly, the next day dancing with craziness,
Dog who needed a couch to figure out his life.
I walked carefully past that freckled beast,
And knew that small things could get you—
Roosters with their spurs,
Spiders with their own poison factories.
I was five. I was wandering the street,
A deflated beach ball tucked under my arm,
And eating apricots. I was looking
For the plug that held the air,
A "stopper," my brother said, the "*cosa*" mother countered.
I had lost it while playing . . . I walked past that dog,
Whose mouth was plugged with a tennis ball,
His own stopper? I spit out an apricot pit.
If the ball fell from his mouth would he slowly shrivel,
Like the beach ball under my arm?
I hurried away, my lips sweetened with
The juice of a summer fruit. I blew mightily in the stem
Of the beach ball. I thought, I'll sock it lightly,
Keep it up in the air with finger pokes,
And juggle it, happy at my genius.
The ball stayed up for a while, then collapsed,
Out of breath. By then the apricots were gone,
And it was near dusk. The light
That reflected off the windows was also gone,
And workers, thin as straw, had left the broom factory.
I watched them march away,
And worried that they could flatten to nothing,
Shadows perhaps on a moist grave.
I kicked my deflated beach ball
Into the street, where it was run over all night.
As for the dog? The tennis ball fell

From his mouth, for he disappeared,
Freckled beast of my childhood.
He must have walked slowly into the weeds,
First wagging his tail, then
His pointy ears falling down in sadness.

No river flowed through the city. Our school was scarred
With graffiti, and bullies peed on our garden project.
I was scared, shoved around.
I lay on the grass in November.
The geese were still with us, plentiful,
Noisy in their honk and wing-beat.
Geese got to fly south, where in the end they'd park
Themselves on a river bank and eat sweet grass.
I chewed a stalk of grass, mused how birds hid,
Brown in the sage, some white against the snow,
Speckled, berry red, blue as juniper,
Dusty as car exhaust. They could leap
From one branch to another, and shift
A single eye on the lookout.
I was musing on my back,
Done chewing my grass,
When the bully from room twelve stood above me,
Hand on his fly. I knew enough to roll
Onto my knees, jump up,
Me the penguin with short wings,
With my black coat, white shirt.
With my clubbed feet waddling backward.
On a cold day, the steam of pee rose
Where I had lain in a city
Where no river flowed from there to the sky.

EVENING ON THE LAWN

I sat on the lawn watching the half-hearted moon rise,
The gnats orbiting the peach pit that I spat out
When the sweetness was gone. I was twenty,
Wet behind the ears from my car wash job,
And suddenly rising to my feet when I saw in early evening
A cloud roll over a section of stars.
It was boiling, a cloud
Churning in one place and washing those three or four stars.
Excited, I lay back down,
My stomach a valley, my arms twined with new rope,
My hair a youthful black. I called my mother and stepfather,
And said something amazing was happening up there.
They shaded their eyes from the porch light.
They looked and looked before my mom turned
The garden hose onto a rosebush and my stepfather scolded the cat
To get the hell off the car. The old man grumbled
About missing something on TV,
The old lady made a face
When mud splashed her slippers. How you bother,
She said for the last time, the screen door closing like a sigh.
I turned off the porch light, undid my shoes.
The cloud boiled over those stars until it was burned by their icy fire.
The night was now clear. The wind brought me a scent
Of a place where I would go alone,
Then find others, all barefoot.
In time, each of us would boil clouds
And strike our childhood houses
With lightning.

With one window of the labor bus gone,
Wind stirred the lunches
Of men with puckered brows.
I looked in my lunch bag—
Five crackers speckled
With salt. I licked my lips
And lapped one of the saltines.
Brother asked, "What are you doing?"
He was holding onto the seat in front
Of him. "Brunch," I said,
Then laughed, *brunch* the one
Word I had learned in English
The previous week. I licked
One side, then the other,
And returned the cracker to my bag,
Soggy from the strapping of my tongue.
Outside, the beet and cotton fields,
And darkness where the sloe-eyed
Headlights didn't cut a path.
When the labor bus bumped over a pothole,
We all screamed. The wind picked up,
Flapping the sleeves of our flannel shirts.
"Rough winds do shake the darling buds
of May," I quoted to the lunch
In my lap. My brother asked,
"What did you say?" Shakespeare,
I answered, this too learned in English,
A line to confuse a girl
In the third row. Brunch
And Shakespeare, and me
Saying "Cheerio, Jeeves" to the bus driver,
With wind still flapping
In his hair. I stepped

Off the bus, lunch under
My arm, and picked up my hoe.
It was beets that day, plants with their arms up
And slaughtered by the time the saltine crackers
Were eaten, by the time
The lucky rich were sitting down
To the lovely morsels of High Tea.

My stepfather said, It's dog-eat-dog,
And wiggled the dining table
When he sawed through the poverty-level pot roast,
Our Sunday meal. Lit from shots of bourbon,
He slurred, Get the other guy first.
I looked over at my brother,
One knee jerking, already nervous
Because the heavy drinking
Would start later during *Bonanza*,
All of us on the floor
And the TV roaring in our ears. I saw
How my brother's hand went into the plastic bag
Of Rainbo Bread,
And rifled past the first three slices,
Starched dry from the air
And not as moist
As those further back. I was still Catholic,
Still stitched up with wings on my back,
And I thought what's wrong
With the first slices? I knew Jesus,
Proprietor of the first soup kitchen,
Handed out loaves on a burnt hill
And loaves at the last supper,
Where Judas, the tricky one,
May have chosen the softest chunk,
May have stolen a fish to place
Between the top and bottom
Of the torn but unshared bread.
At our house we played out the last supper
As we waited for our stepfather
To fall over, dead. But he buttered
His slice, drank his brew,
And warned, First come first served.

You were not going to
Make it—even here, within the four
Walls moist from scared breathing—
If you didn't learn to shove
A hand into the plastic bag
And reach way back, for the best.
At supper, he said this, and more,
With a tender chunk of meat on his fork.
He died of a bad heart—
It was dog-eat-dog.

The best-looking women married five times.
The sorrowful ones married once, and stayed the course,
Shoring up shadows under their eyes.
One of the babes flew over on the flutter of eyelashes,
Deforested from twenty-three years of crying. Gary, she cried,
And I said, Martha! The babe propped her hands
On her hips. She pouted. Sara, I tried. Becky! Virginia!
My memory was a shoreline eaten by waves. I was offering
Her the consolation of a beer
When a crow landed on her beehive hairdo,
A relic from the sixties. The babe pulled at her hair
And ran, a small dog snapping at her sandals.
In two wing-beats, the crow flew onto the garage roof.
I thought, *The Birds*. Alfred Hitchcock. Tipi Hedren
And Suzanne Pleshette dragged onto her porch by sparrows.
But Fresno had no shore or lighthouse,
No famous actress, no sea breeze to speak of.
We had rage. Here each of us citizens had eaten a bird
And were ready to peck the eyes of our enemies.
When the babe returned, her hairdo leaning,
I said, Are you OK, sugar?
She smiled, fingertips applauding: Oh, you remember!
I popped open a beer, my first. *Pues sí*, I said,
And recalled they called her Dulce or Sugar.
But the sweetness was long gone, licked by her first husband.
I looked toward the roof, the TV antenna fallen over.
Two crows were wiping their beaks under the rags
Of their wings. The backyard scene was a junior high dance.
Crow was dinner. Later, for a snack in a parked car,
I nibbled the buttons of her blouse
Until my teeth were flossed with thread,
And lowered my face into her neck,
My poor tongue swollen from the salt of her working years.

STOCK MARKET

1.

I bet my wad on rubber bands
And every stock went up but mine.
Immediately I was pushing a shopping cart.
The glorious west was done for me. My neighbor's dog, Fluffy,
Was at my side. Twin failures, we followed the dark
Wind of an industrial alley and stopped to iron out a pothole
With my shoe. Fluffy used the pads
Of her soft paws. For good measure,
I jumped three times on my handiwork—
My contribution to society. I then gave my attention
To a pigeon pumping its claws up and down,
Feathered-friend with chewing gum gluing him in place.
I picked up that poor creature, its beak stringy with gum,
And whispered where I thought his ear might be,
Everyone bought gold but me.
Fluffy barked. She knew this was true.
I thrust my hands into my cart and brought up handfuls of rubber bands.
I was rich with ignorance. I worked forty-seven rubber bands
Around my wrist and said to the bird, The blood flow is cut off,
And I can't draw no more. Or write. Or work
My bow over the strings of a warped violin.
I saw myself in the shiny territory of the pigeon's eyes,
My nose mountainous, my nostril hairs a frightening forest.

The sun bled behind a cloud. The telephone wires swung in the wind,
The once high-and-mighty kites charred to sticks.
I hugged the derelict pigeon,
Then cleaned his face and claws,
Yet another contribution to society.
The pigeon fluttered skyward
But not far. Instead, he preferred to walk,
With me a proper distance behind his crutchlike steps,

With me shooting his tail with my arsenal of rubber bands.
I picked up chewing gum on the bottoms of my shoes,
A workout because I had to raise my steps high
To get anywhere. I had tried the stock market
And lost. And where my gummed-up friend, Fluffy, and I were going,
Neither feathers nor fur nor skin mattered much.
We had used up our luck.
We kicked and clawed at the hungry earth,
Potholes opening for one more feeding.

2.

The pigeon was a Buddha, one foot in the rivulet
And the other on a rock. I said to Fluffy, The bird knows more than us.
At this the Buddha bird warbled. Was this his sermon on the mount?
The god of the street thrust his beak under his wing
And brought out a flea. With that,
I hurried away without my shopping cart,
Undoing the rubber bands from my wrist. My hand was white
From that pressure, and the carpal gates opened again,
Blood bathing the cells that throbbed for more drink.
I raised my hand skyward
And then let it swing at my side.
I had enough of the alley. The sun
Was no more than an ember at the alley's end.
When a dog barked, and Fluffy sniffed the air,
A lathe in one of the warehouses started
And stopped. I counted up my losses—money
And love, foothill property where ducks clacked their bills
For the pleasure of pulling grass from a murky pond.
A second dog barked. Fluffy ignored her natural call.
I had departed with a shopping cart
Of rubber bands, my heist from the stock market,
And now I was watching my breath,
A pastime when you have nothing.
I was rubbing my once-dead hand and pulling on each finger

When a warehouse slammed shut, startling me.
Something was over, done with, the day shift
Walking away with oiled faces. On a fence,
A cat was carrying a pigeon in its mouth.
The pigeon struggled, its claws spread like roots.
My breath broke apart. My fists opened and closed.
I was the dying territory a bird's begging eye.

That don't sell! the gray wig yelled,
His teeth gone from biting the asses of tardy employees.
This much I was told
After I had gotten my math wrong on the first day
As a broker on the trading floor.
My bow tie was bent.
The hairs on my ears smelled of sawdust.
Yet, I lectured: the grass bends and so must we, my fellow brokers.
Nah, your story has an old beard, another chief scolded
When I ended my speech—
My voice had the thrust of a gnat working its wings
Through a screened door. I wiped my mouth
And tried again.
But the moneymakers of the Dow patted their bellies.
They yawned when I said the camel will sleep in the eye
Of the needle before the rich man
Votes Democrat. My biblical message
Was contorted, but they got my meaning.

Heroes of change were dead. Jesus went first,
And went again when the people
Called him back for more of the same.
I was called once. I made my pitch for the limping poor,
My wings halfway through that screened door,
And was then led down the noiseless hall,
The potted plants all at attention. No telling
When the boss would call for cost-effective measures
And have the rhododendron dragged away
By its leafy ears.

The cabdriver watched me from across the street.
He sucked on a water bottle, then drove away,
Two nonpaying flies in the back window.
The curb was painted red—blood of a sorrowful brother?
I imagined him knocked down and getting up, not godlike,
But with the stamina of a burro. I imagined the spark
Of his hooves as he headed to the Westside,
The edge of the filthy sky burning like a curtain.
I crossed the street. The cracked speaker
Was trying to tell me something. Any other day
It would have been music. Now the voice
Was saying, You got a job for me? I looked up
To the speaker, once used to splash the air with music,
But now a public address system. Then I remembered
The curb, hurried over to that marked place,
And discovered not blood but city paint,
A warning not to park—let alone stand—there
Especially on a Friday night. The curtain was burning.
The *paleta* carts were jiggling a last call.
The mall was closing up. Even the Hispanic preacher
With the weight of centuries in his brow
Was going home. Like Jesus, he'd had his say,
And the speaker, at tree level, was trying me again—
You got a job, man? A hot wind howled
Between buildings. I felt a coin
In my pocket and tossed it into the fountain,
The water's corrosive powers ready to dissolve the face
Of the American buffalo.

The goats chewed in sunlight,
Their ancient beards touching the valley floor.
Shadows fidgeted over granite rocks and tree stumps.
Rabbits kicked themselves in the manzanita,
And in the brush crickets rattled their thighs.
I wiped my brow and thought, This ain't me.
A week before a bud and I imagined that we might trek
Where John Muir had trekked, his own beard sweeping
The valley floor, hike in early morning
And discover a hilly rise. From that vista,
We'd pronounce one philosophical thing or another,
Then carry happiness like water in our cupped palms—
Much of it spilling between our fingers,
But some of it coming back with us. But we found out
There was no water, no, indeed, only salt mines under our arms.
I slapped the soulless gnats from my face,
The little devils on wings. After an hour,
I said to my bud, Is this the rise?
When we came to a steep climb. He licked his lips
And said, John Muir weighed only a hundred and thirty.
I said, Ben Franklin said God meant for men to drink beer.
My bud licked his lip. How so? he asked.
I bent my arm three times
And said, The elbow is like a hinge, brother.
I motioned my hand to my face.
But there was no beer, no John or Ben, no answer to whether
From this dusty rise sprang happiness.
I sat down on a stump. Goats bleated down below,
Some of the older ones perched on granite rocks.
One slip, and their hooves would have sparked a fire
And burned the grass in their mouths.
I considered the goats and my hands,
Dry ravines. There was no happiness for me.

I was tired, used up. My jealous friends were those bugs
Seething when you lifted a rock. I lifted a rock—
They were there. The wind brought me not kites or flowers
But the smell of a dead jay with its legs like spurs
And its juices long gone.

At fifty, the excitement recedes.
What of the twin tulip bulbs in the damp February earth,
The calfskin shiny as copper, the last wave sustained by the shark's blood,
The pitiful fountain, the ant embarking on its leaf in the spray?

What of the dolphin-sleek women on the beach,
The flat rock flung over water and water,
The tree that unbuttons its leaves in October,
And sun, imperial crown, ripening one side of plums.

What of the childhood photos with your head cut off,
The lost sweetness of gum on the back molar,
The sea that scrubbed your back, the moon that lit your eyes,
The love that came running when you called her name?

What of the pencil lead under your writing hand,
The uppercase alphabet of craziness,
The comma that's a paring from a chewed fingernail,
The sentence that's a snail with its tape measure of silence?

Time is an egg, with the pinprick of a hole,
The puddled goo on the kitchen's drain board.
One wipe of a dirty sponge,
And we're gone.

When I died, my work went into my mother's attic.
Spiders climbed onto my still lifes
And a rat ate my name from the corner.
One time a woman in a restaurant said my name, Giacomo.
Another time a blind man hungered for color
And crawled along a ditch bank,
Calling my name into the midnight blue.

My mother died with a crochet hook in her hands.
Light spilled like milk onto her face
And was sucked into her pale eyelids.
The color of ash, her body was carried from the house
To become ash and fill the wind with an awful gray.

My canvases were hidden from the Germans.
Battles were fought and lost,
Love made and undone on soiled beds.
Then my portraits were discovered by a janitor,
Who carried three pieces home.
He said to a surviving son, The artist cut off his nose,
And maybe a portion of his ear,
Plus his heart passed through his liver—
He drank himself into the poorhouse.

Snow felled a tree, and the summer's sun raised it back up.
The boy was now a young man.
He recognized hunger when a mouse climbed the wall
And ate an apple from one of the still lifes.
The young man shivered. He chewed a button
From his coat and tasted the road's salt,
Rain, and the splash of wine from the night before.
He swallowed that button: Art is the last thing
Left to eat.

DIRT
apologies to Wallace Stevens

The philosopher says, The soil is man's intelligence,
And if so, then we are smarter than any tweedy prof,
We with the hoes, the horizon flat wherever we turn.
The sun comes up angry. The wind bullies us from behind,
And as we space beet plants with tiny golf swings
I say to my brother in the next row,
We're smarter than you think.
He looks up with his dirty face—
What are you talking about?
And I answer with a laugh,
Say, as I slaughter two more plants,
I got me two sandwiches to eat. How 'bout you?
My brother pleats his brow, tells me to shut up—
I do. The wind pushes,
The sun's half-wafer of light reddens.
A dog's bark echoes from the canal
Where workers will later wash their feet at the day's end.
I'm glad to be by my brother,
Glad for this education in the Big Bosses' skinny rows.
I chop my beets, keep my mouth closed.
I think to myself, I'm in college,
I'm in this field where crows follow me like guards.
I'm thinking of the philosopher dead thirty years
And covered smartly in the same ancient dirt
Lifted and falling from my hoe.

WANTING TO GO BACK HOME

The parakeet meets me at the back door,
And spits out its seed. It walks toward me,
Bird the size of a hammered thumb.
"What?" it asks. "What? What?"
This bruise-colored bird lifts a claw,
Drops it, and flutters onto the kitchen table
Where there's a plastic bag
Of bread, a single pencil,
Three marbles. The parakeet dips
Its head and walks bravely into
The plastic bag. When I look in,
The bird is gone. The curtain lifts,
And I think that it's flown
Out the window. But
It's only wind stirring the scent of iron
From the junkyard next door.
A dog drags its chain, a diesel brakes.
I sit in a chair, both hands
On the table like gavels. The bag
That swallowed the parakeet
Is gone, now the pencil,
Two of the three marbles.
When the wind raises
The curtain, I look up and outside.
I'm losing what I loved best—
Sunlight on a Saturday
When, age five, I rolled on my back
And was already thinking
Of the past. I want to go back—God,
To pet the head of a closed-eyed parakeet
And to roll that last marble
Between my fingers,
Marble that is sightless,
Scratched, and speckled
Wet from years of rain.

PART TWO
Film treatments for David Lynch

The girl we all loved married a meatpacker in Hayward,
Not once but twice. The first go-around,
She complained of the stink of blood,
Though Larry, her hubby, washed his hands in the garden hose
Before he entered and yelled, Yoohoo, I'm home.
The second time around his right hand was severed
When it traveled like a salmon into the wrapping machine.
She cooed, Poor Baby. Lawyers, marbled as steaks,
Appeared at his door. The settlement
Was used up in six months,
And now they faced each other in a trailer park,
Each complaining about the cost of barbecued pork rinds,
Free when Larry worked at the meat factory.
Now rib eye, tri-tips, ground round, butt roast all cost dearly,
Hotdogs, too, plus jerky and Slim Jims.
These days they had no meat to scent the air with blood,
And Larry had only one hand to scratch his head
And ask himself, What happened? But Larry was a character,
A wiseass who did handstands on his stump
For children to see. But he wasn't finished there. No,
Larry was a magician with his appendage,
The filmy sweat at the sewn end gluey enough
To pick up nickels and dimes from the street,
Bobby pins, bottle caps, crayons melted from the sun.
He thought, I could be on afternoon TV!
His stump was a meaty magnet when he invited over
A couple in Hawaiian shirts. A show-off,
He willed the weight of a chrome cigarette lighter
To stay glued when he picked it up from the table,
These friends clapping with their two hands.
But the girl we all loved only yawned,
Her tongue shiny as shrink-wrapped salmon.
The couples drove off to dine at Denny's,

Where forks and spoons flew into his stump,
He the living Swiss Army knife.
They ate burgers and chicken, and talked some,
Their chests were deflated but their bellies were full.
The two couples swigged iced teas. The waitress
Arrived with the check. I ain't good
At paper, Larry told his buddy across from him.

To prove his point, Larry stabbed at his napkin,
Matches, a business card,
An old bowling score from his shirt pocket.
Something about paper,
Something about no dollars in his wallet.
The husband of the girl we all loved
Couldn't pick up the check.

Marvin, penny-pincher, seller of red velour to Mexicans,
Cut his own lawn. This despite the five pounds
Of nickels in his pockets. This despite the stocks
In a shoe box and the ashes of his wife, too, in a cookie tin.
Her yakkity-yak was still the voice on the answering machine,
And her terrier, Fluffy, lived on.
Marvin wiped his face. He bent over the two-stroke engine
Of his lawn mower and poured gas into its tank.
But the gas hit the hot manifold and a slap of flames
Lit Marvin's tie. He staggered back, brushing the fire
From his chest, a collapsed empire of muscle.
He could have rubbed his wife's ashes into his eyes.
But he didn't have time for that. He staggered
In his yard, a quickly kindled Christmas tree,
And jumped into the kidney-shaped pool, blue as toilet wash.
The flames were gone and now he struggled for air.
The nickels pulled him down. His wig floated off like an island.
His hearing aids popped out and settled like snails
On the bottom of the pool. His dentures had their last say,
Three large bubbles discharged from the molars.
But the remnants of his empire of muscles
Rose gallantly and hoisted him to the edge.
He breathed and breathed. The sky was bluer than
He remembered. Fluffy waddled to the edge.
Oh, how Marvin was happy, only a few nickels
Lost, though retrievable at the end of fall
When the pool was drained. Then Fluffy's anger flared up
Like gasoline on a hot manifold and nibbled
None-too-nicely Marvin's gripping fingers.
The master salesman of layaway furniture cried once
And lost his grip. Fluffy rubbed her itchy bottom
From one end of the lawn to the other,
Done with that man—Marvin shitting his pants

As he descended, eyes bulged as he witnessed
Nickels spilling from his pockets.
Turds floated on water, even in a rich man's pool.

Only an hour ago fog washed over a dusty Lincoln
And the dead man inside, his cheek bone a starburst of blood.
Fog cleaned nothing. Wind through the cracked window
Fluttered the map in the dead man's grip, but he wasn't going anywhere
But down. That wouldn't be for weeks.
First, his yawn widened
And his tongue filled with a dam of unspeakable words.
Second, ants discovered the jelly behind his eyes.
Third, a dog barked. Fourth, a car stopped
And the driver took pictures, then pulled away.
The fog returned with the acids of an industrial laundry
Two miles from the dead man who, when alive, drove past it,
His own shirt starched, his pants done right.
His real estate empire of two apartment buildings was gone,
As were the thick-throated cries from his wife, his stocks
And savings, the young man he played ball with on Saturdays.
He pouted, They'll be sorry. He pouted a long face
When he was nine and at sixty-nine. Now the fog
Washed over the Lincoln at the edge of the remote cove.
No one came. Fifth, a plane portioned up the sky with its exhaust.
Sixth, a bulldozer removed rocks from the rain-soaked cliff.
Yet he remained, dead in his car,
Though one union worker put down his meaty sandwich
And asked, You smell something?
The hard hats sniffed the air. Just grass, they said,
And licked mustard from the lug nuts of their knuckles.
The creases in the dead man's shirt unfolded
As he slumped over from the trembling
Of idling bulldozers.

This is Mr. Powell, his mustache twitching,
And this is Mrs. Powell, the roots of her hair coming through.
A double suicide. Mr. Powell went first, followed
By his wife, who screamed into a tape recorder, He can't show me up!
I beat him fair and square at bowling,
And he didn't think I saw him with a second bag of peanuts!

This is Mrs. Gamez, the rats of cancer in both breasts.
This is Tony, with a syringe still attached at the back of his leg.
And this is Mrs. Welch, a washout as the Fat Lady in a traveling circus.
Here is the boy whose head was crushed when the jack fell off its stand,
Boy now with a head flat as a business card.

This is Jamal, and this is Enrique, unclaimed tags on their toes.
None of them will stay. Take drawer number sixteen,
A girl with the smudges of madness on her lips.
She'll go soon. Her neighbor with six nose rings will go,
And the murdered crackhead popped with a .22 soon rolls away.
The clipboard tells the truth: one of us is missing, ourselves of course—
You now stepping into the shower,
You the next asshole shooting off your mouth in the Cram-It-In Eatery.
But first the truly bad female impersonator
And then the sausage maker who ground his arm into bankruptcy.
Let's bring on the CEO of Greed, the Master Sergeant of Bad Behavior.
Let Macho Man fly into the radiator of an oncoming produce truck.

The art of dying. Color is drained from the faces of retirees
And pushed into bluish toes. The drawers open and close,
Making room for the itinerant dead, all with eyes shut,
Though the young ones—pill heads,
Spike-headed punks—still giddy, sometimes peek.
Later, the bravest mourners will kiss them closed.

The dead man lay with a plum in his throat. His left hand
Held a pen, its vein of ink nearly gone.
His right hand gripped his mortgage papers.
Water dripped in the kitchen sink. But that was no clue,
Neither were the worn slippers on his feet.
The Detective tipped back his hat. He had seen the dead
In many postures and this fellow was nothing new.
He had seen the dead lodged in chimneys,
The adulterous dead caught in the outstroke of lovemaking.
Drowned men sunk in rivers and buoyed up with their bellies full
Of moonlight and murky water. Yes,
After many years, the Detective understood the map of bloodstains
And the victims starched by justified fear. That's how he saw
Those who succumbed on a wet Thursday. It was Thursday now,
Though dry. A crime was involved. The Detective,
Breathing on a window, noted a splotch the size of a newborn's head.
But that evidence would fade soon. So would the last pinprick
Of red in the man's red cheek. The Detective knelt
And rolled the man's head back and forth—no, no was the answer.
He wrote this much in a notebook. He whittled away time,
Tapping his pencil on his thigh. Time had stopped
For this man, age forty-nine, on the floor. That his fingernails would continue
Was a given. But how would he claw his way out of the morgue,
Once he was fitted on a tray and rolled into darkness?
And what if they turned him onto his belly
And they dislodged the plum pit? It was an open-and-shut case
That he lived and died, and had signed on the line
At Dot.Com Savings and Loan. The wind whistled
When the door opened. The men with latex gloves were here,
Wiser by one more day: don't suck a plum pit
With a pen in one hand, a thirty-year mortgage in the other.

The skateboarder with blackheads ran into a wall.
The child in a wheelchair let go of her balloon
And the sky ate its redness. Dogs hugged hedges
After two cars leaped curbs and crushed a row of saplings.
It was a dangerous Thursday. Christ would hang on Friday,
And atheists would stay home, among them
Mr. Salvador Rios, who hollered at the skateboarder
And gleefully watched the balloon disappear. He laughed at Christians,
He laughed at Jews. Mr. Rios read the newspaper
And why Jesus was not in the obituaries was the true mystery,
For that ancient died over and over. He believed in prunes
And a short evening walk that released pockets of gas
When he stepped onto curbs. He believed in port,
Two small glasses to burst fat from his heart.
He gave nothing, took nothing. He wiped his mouth
Because it was his own. It was Thursday.
Tomorrow people in nice clothes would feel sorrow.
But first they would gas up their SUVs for the weekend—
Egg hunts for snotty children who taste yolk when the shell is broken,
Yolk and not the sweetness of candy. They let go their balloons
That explode, like faith, before they reach untouchable heaven.

The police found an arm and foot in a zipped-up gym bag,
Then a torso and three fingers in another.
A black bird perched on the head two miles away,
Head on a pile of hard pan no rain could rinse into gold.
The severed parts appeared in a canal. The piecework began
Where the frogs had gone quiet, their spiteful tongues gathering goo.
This was a Thursday-night murder
Under a fishbowl sky. The rookie cop saluted his captain.
He bagged these bloodless body parts
And lay them on a metal table with one of its wheels gone.
His job done, the rookie circled the block in his cruiser
For that crime and others. He did what he was told,
A half-eaten burger in his lap, french fries the length of fingers.
Then he saw: pedestrians had hatchets in their stares,
Anger in the black and white punks, the Korean liquor store owners,
The Pakistani cabdrivers, the Mexican gardeners on their knees,
And the middle-aged yoga teacher, her contorted legs behind her head,
Nearly severed from her body by the look of things.
The rookie swallowed his cold burger.
He sped up his cruiser: in the rearview mirror,
He followed the arc of knives and hatchets hurled at him—
Tomahawks of hatred from the mailman
And poorly dressed social worker,
The giddy-up college students on scooters.
His breathing rushed. A homeless woman buried a fork
In his forehead. With each blink,
The spot of blood behind his eyes flashed.
At a red light, he brushed french fries from his lap,
Fingers, he thought, burnt fingers
Falling and the bodies long gone.

The severed forearm stands like a sapling in the river's mud.
The police dog's tooth floats under the left arm of a rapist.
The pornographer with his blow-up doll eats potato chips on a couch.
The underpants of the pastor's wife cling drying to a bush.
The young English prof lifts three academic lines from the French
And his molars collide guiltily at the first faculty meeting in autumn.

The clues mount. The days are chewed by the angry
And their juices flood the street. If he could,
Neighbor A would chase Neighbor B with his lawn mower,
But his tie is on, his Volvo idling with his child buckled in.
There is madness in the anorectic nun's fear of swallowing her own saliva.
There is sanity in God's wafer on the roof of a child's mouth.
There is beauty in the head of lettuce with ice at its core.

The last good man peels a hard-boiled egg at his sink.
He's happy. No one likes him. The weather is cruel,
Men worse. The eggshells are white as snow
But jagged as razors when raked across a cheek.
The envious think the worst and receive it by evening—
The eggs they break drool blood in a batter of lopsided cakes.

While the moon stirred the trees, not a single leaf let go.
But bras were undone, panties kicked off, the flagship of cocks
Surfaced from underwear. But it stopped there
For adolescent boys with a pimple on each side
Of their flared nostrils. These boys were not going to get
Their way. Neither were the dogs who tossed their water bowls
And howled for their share of pork chop bones.
The world was stubborn on a regular Thursday
When newspapers sailed onto pitched roofs.
Goldfish spat up their flakes. Cats refused to be smoked out
Of chimneys. Garbage collectors kicked over trash cans
And yelled, Pick up your own shit! Miss Blue Blood
Wrote in her column, Ladies, melt down
Your rings and get out of town. Thus the silence.
Thus the men who gnawed a round steak down to the marrow.
I noticed this loneliness. I noticed Fluffy, my neighbor's dog,
Following me at shadow's length on my trek around the block.
But I wagged my head. I was out to track the moon,
Its pull so strong that my hobo beard was horizontal.
We men were not going to get our way. This much was clear.
Earlier, my own mustard bottle failed to give up its goo,
No matter how hard I squeezed over my hotdog,
And the answering machine cut off a poolside starlet from Hollywood.
And now on my street men were bathed in the orange runoff
Of their porch lights. Some still clung to their steak bones,
Sucked dry, and beer cans were scattered on the lawns.
Now that our wives were gone, our bodies were wet
From the fury of scouring rice stuck to the bottoms of pots.
It was a Thursday. I had no answers
For the moon pulling my beard like a leash.
I was tied to something larger, like love.
The streetlights pooled their brightness

Onto the black asphalt, which we—lost men
On all fours like dogs—crawled, the gravity
Of years lowering the sacks under our desperate eyes.

The palm reader viewed a child's death
In the rearview mirror. No, she was mistaken.
There was no child with a sack lunch in his hand.
A truck had burst through a dirty mattress
At the side of the road. There was nothing to report,
Via the rearview mirror, or her cards, or the milky fog
Stirring at ground level. And what of the tea leaves
And the lines of fortune on an idiot's palm?
She pressed the gas pedal. Autumn had arrived
Two weeks late, the geese tired of the old game
Of flying south. Last night's wind broke limbs,
Crazed chickens, and rippled the surface
Of irrigation ditches of failed farms. Apples fell,
All with the question marks of worms at their center.

The palm reader was losing her skill.
She foretold the ugly man's marriage,
A father's reunion with his son, the rise of the stock market
Just after lunch—somewhere a broker reached across
His desk and passed gas, the helium of his odorous body
Stirring nothing in the Dow. She was losing faith,
Like the geese who were stopping in Texas.
Jewelry banged on her wrists
When she flipped a card, and her own hand
Became a swamp of nervousness when she started,
You will marry . . . Often they were married,
Or gay, or more fascinated with money
Than a would-be husband with a hearing aid.

The palm reader parked the car in her drive.
The house was silent, but her purse made noise
When she tossed it on the coffee table—the hearing aid
Of her ex-husband rolled onto the carpeted floor.
Rat! she wanted to scream at the device

The color of an artificial leg. He had run off
With a dental hygienist, he a man with fewer
Than a dozen teeth in his head. She turned on the TV.
The president's face appeared larger than life.
There may be war, he said, there may be peace.

She thought: Oh, God, he's worse than me!
Today she guessed a child's death
In the rearview mirror, guessed a happy marriage
In a fan of cards for a middle-aged couple.
She would have to wait for the late news to hear about them,
The couple who held hands when they left her office
But later at home slew each other with insults
Before the rifles came off the wall.

PHYSICAL FOR THE FIFTY-FIVE-AND-OVER RETIREMENT COMMUNITY

You're in great shape, said the nurse,
And I asked, What part?

She told me to strip off my shirt,
Flag of defeat that hid my chest and belly,
Two once-great empires dissipated into provinces.

She held up my arm, flaccid snake on an old trunk,
And narrowed her eyes,
The pinched mouth of a tailor with a needle in his teeth.

You're only as old as you feel, she said.
She smoothed the back of my arm near my shoulder,
Only visible to me when I look in the mirror,
Barely reachable when I soap my body.
I twisted my neck trying to see what she saw,
An unnameable anatomy, not like teeth or nose,
Chin or cheek bones riding the crest of noble beauty.

I touched the back of my arm,
Skin to graft on the burned part of my writing hand.
And I was burning then, the shame of having nothing left,
Just skin with the shrinking territory of a half-dollar,
A quarter, a dime, the diminishing value
Of an old man with shrubbery hanging from his nose.

My realtor friend says, The house is haunted.
The owner died in a hot tub, his wife in a lounge chair.
The middle child collapsed with his head in the stove.
And the dog, a bothersome yakker poisoned one night,
Is buried in the yard. The yard is overgrown with weeds
And berry bushes. Crickets and mosquitoes thrive,
And turd-colored toads multiply daily by fours and fives.
I flick on the light switch in the den
And the darkness lays crumbled like a body on the floor.
The room is airless. Dust doesn't climb more than an inch before it falls.
What's that? I ask of the bolts on the wall. My realtor friend smirks.
For your pleasure, he says, and flicks an invisible whip. I picture
A portly man in a leather thong, flinching before the whacking begins,
His mouth terrorized with three shades of lipstick.
His cock is holstered in a leather pouch.
Jesus, I say, and I ask, So this is Beverly Hills?
My friend smiles and shows me the master bedroom,
Where, he says, the dead circulate and knock in the walls.
I picture the dead with their dead pooch. They ask repeatedly,
Who did this to us, Fluffy? They're sitting on the bed's edge,
The husband and wife, the son with his lungs basted with gas.
The dead go away, come back, go away with nothing to report.
How much for this place? I ask my realtor friend,
Who licks a thumb and flips through his clipboard.
With so many dead, with these spirits weeping at night,
A pretty penny. A high for the producer, the director,
A high for the once-pretty faces with everything,
The car, the ski rack on the car, three homes in two countries,
Everything except talent and a place inside them for a soul.

PART THREE

Why would anyone—lost child, thief,
Homeless anemic in his rags—
Want to climb into my apartment,
While I, Gil Mendez, twice-married soul,
Have been trying to climb out the window
And walk for good across my dead lawn,
My footsteps small as the hooves
Of a burro, evidence that we wear down
Not only the flint that sparks from the heart
But the feet as well? I couldn't figure
A poor soul climbing in an opened window,
And me in my darkened bedroom
With a twirl of reincarnated flies,
Or was it the vortex
Of boredom from which all yawns stir?
Yes, I thought, I was doing no more than
Shaking a small transistor radio,
For the batteries were good, nearly new,
For I bought them along with a pack of razors,
And weren't they still in a drawer
In the bathroom, steamy because
I had just showered and shaved,
Clipped my toenails. Yes, this near burglary
Occurred as I was seated on the edge
Of my bed, thumbing the dial
Of my radio—come in Mexicali,
Bring me news Coachella Valley,
Sing to my dinky Del Rey of the girl
Who washed her man's face
With her hair, then sent him off,
His ribs bruised from the continual slap
Of her brown thighs.
I considered the window

And how, really, I hadn't slammed it down
But the wind, yes, it was the wind
That shimmied the frame and set
The window falling, guillotine-like,
On four fingers. The man screamed, "*Ay!*"
Then with his free hand he lifted the window
And ran off, weaving between
The chickens in the yard. After that,
I stood in the doorway, eyes spooked,
And heaving up ridges of veins.
Who would want anything from these rooms,
This haven for dust and spiders?
Hangers bang in the closet,
The mattress bleeds sweat in this hottest of months,
And the bread crumbs march
Across the kitchen table
When the fan swings their way,
Crumbs that were once whole
But now like me, scattered,
An old man holding a radio
And no one singing.

*

If you wake slowly in Fresno,
Lie in bed while a herd of rats scuttle in the ceiling,
Then you miss the sun
With its old trick—how lovely
It looks at 6:32, the sun over the sycamores,
Panties like flowers on a clothesline,
And saucy cats licking their glory.
But by 10:39, you who work with shovels
And an oily wrench, you who pull ladders
To plum trees, you who stir the black
Pitch that slobbers the holes on roofs,
Flat and angled—you know

How the feet sink in the swamp water
Of sweat . . . I drink water
And, yes, I thought, Today is the day
To collect what is owed me. But first
I studied my lawn, its roots the nerve ends of death,
A place to stretch out in the evenings.
I plucked the wilted flower off my geranium bush.
I kicked sand at the chickens
In the yard—illegal in the city—
Then set off to collect eighteen dollars
From a man—good God, I thought—
With my own first name. Gilberto
Hernandez, thin as an earthworm,
Has the personality of an earthworm,
Silent and flatulent, the air about him
Like something cows bring
To the barn. I thought, I'm collecting money
From myself—the left hand
Is asking the right hand, Please pay,
Because I've got to buy bread and a can of soup.
I walked down Tulare Street,
Asking myself, What if Gilberto
Isn't home, then what? Would I
Have walked three miles to rap
On a door and shoo a fly from my face?
As it happened, I never arrived
To collect this debt.
I gasped for air, for any kind of luck,
As I made out my approaching nephew, Walter,
Idiotic boy with the guitar itself like a hump on his back.
At his side, a brown dog ran,
Its happiness something glorious,
For a petal of tongue hung from its mouth.
There must be some mistake, I thought—
My nephew now singing with a dog?
I assessed my shoes, two leather boats;

I was sweaty from this walk.
Exhausted, the sun wouldn't let me be,
Persecuting sun who has the heights
Over us lowly citizens.
On this short walk I whittled twenty-five minutes
From my bony life, all
Because I had the nerve, no, the position,
To ask Gilberto Hernandez for my money,
Owed to me since I tightened my belt by one hole,
Owed to me for we shook hands
And said, "*Adios, carnal.*"
I touched the small of my back, its spur of hurt
From carrying crates in my youth,
Or was it that single affair with a heavy woman,
What was it, thirteen years ago?
I leaned against an ash tree
And closed my eyes.
For the moment, I had seen enough.

*

That afternoon, my nephew Walter thrust a dog
On me, an ugly pooch named Humo,
Whose owner—my nephew's boss,
A gardener, of all things!—had been deported
To Mexico. How I scolded my nephew:
¡Tonto! Illegals are supposed
To work for us, not the other
Way around. But did he listen?
No, he swung his guitar
Onto his back, smiled his cloud-blank smile,
And promised to return with a tattoo on the inside
Of his lip, a "W" for his name
Ay, Dios, I moaned when he relaxed his tongue,
A shiny chrome ball at its center.
What is with the *chavalos* pushing

Nuts and bolts through their metal skin?
At sixty-five, I wished for the solitude
Of my apartment, a rosebush standing watch
In one corner, a geranium in the other,
Sunlight on both of them, a lovely balance
For the living. I wished for the dirt
In my yard, also a balance,
My patch of tomatoes and chilies,
Green beans, squash like huge trumpets.
I wished for the solitude of a cricket in weeds.
Now this dog followed me from room
To room, the petal of his tongue blooming.
His tail wagged, fleas marched
With ancient plague in his fur.
I worried about my nephew—
What young woman would press
Her mouth to a young man's mouth
And taste a chrome ball on her tongue?
What woman would swivel earrings
Clockwise and place a kiss
On his cheek lanced with metal,
The torture of shrapnel in flesh?
After Walter left, I cried, Oh, Dolores, my sister!
Poor sister who lay in a mowed cemetery
With rocks in her eyes. I threw my arms into the air,
But no god caught them.

*

Humo lay near the water heater.
I blew on my tea. On its surface,
I saw the rivulets of lines around an old man's mouth.
I wiped my mouth, but the rivulets remained.
I scolded, Who is your master?
Earlier, Humo had wet the rug
And I yanked him by his collar

Onto the back porch.
I smeared his snout into the rug.
He sneezed twice, dumb dog,
The barometer of his tail still wagging.
Didn't he understand his punishment?
I said: You don't know pain.
My son from my first marriage,
He died when he put his rake
Into the air. I raised my arms
And continued: My poor son
Burned when the rake touched
The power line thirteen years ago,
On an autumn when a blimp was sailing
Over Fresno, poor city bored out of its wits,
With everyone out of their houses saying,
Oh, it's so big. My son was in the yard,
Blisters on his palms from shoveling
Holes for a new fence. Excited
At the appearance of a blimp,
He climbed our roof, laughing
I can bring down the blimp with my rake.
And his body jumped—electricity strikes deep
In the heart, the spleen, the kidney…
My thoughts passed like a blimp, all air and shadow.

I drank my tea, wiped my eyes.
Humo wagged his tail, searched his paw
For a flea. He didn't make me happy.
I asked: Who is your master?
He gets deported
And my son, from this country,
From a woman born in this country, is dead.
How the dumb dog wagged its tail.
I lowered my head onto the tabletop
And listened to the roar inside laminated wood,
This the sound of the afterlife

As far as I am concerned—roar of voices
Wanting to climb out of that tabletop.
Oh, how much a table
Can tell us, I thought, and looked up,
Water in my eyes. I imagined
A rain-speckled window
With no kitchen light behind it.
Dog, I said, I don't know what I am saying.
It's all the blimp's fault.
I wiped my eyes again. I said, OK,
You can stay, but stay away
From the chickens. I peered out the window—
Chickens in a cage, rooster
And a hen pecking the ground.
Between my cottage and Blanca's cottage,
We two holdouts in a place
That would be bulldozed
At the end of the year. I thought:
That's what's between us,
A rooster and a hen. Humo barked
When I stood up. We faced each other,
Old man and new dog.
Who is your master? I asked again,
And Humo kicked a leg into his face,
The fleas having shifted under
The glossy fur. I said, *Ven,* ´
And the dog beat me to the door.
In the yard, Blanca Arroyo,
My neighbor, stood by a rosebush,
Calling, *Señor*, you dropped these!
She held up my underwear
Cut from the line by the night breeze.
¡Ay, Dios! I called as I imagined
My underwear pitched by the wind,
My socks and shirts, all assembled in the air
And dancing about like bats. I hurried away,

My shoes squeaking pitifully.
When I looked back,
Blanca was waving that embarrassing article of clothing,
A sort of surrender? Was she a widow
Ready to swing her own underwear
In her free hand? How much she,
The widow, wanted me,
Though my jowls dripped on my face,
Though my eyes seeped like twilight in a window.
Blanca picked up after me,
Smoothed my sheets on the line,
Readjusted shirts and pants.
She touched them, perhaps longingly
Because she stomped her foot more than once
And cooed, I have soup if you want!
Presently, she waved and smiled
Between a rooster and a hen for the pot.

*

My wives and second son were dead,
My sister Dolores was dead.
For me, an occasional believer,
God was not far behind,
God with his potato peeler
And the scraped world in his soft hands.
I walked with the dog at my side,
Past homes set far from the street,
Half-hidden in shadow
Now that the sun had fallen
Just behind the leafy trees.
I bent down over a girl with chalk
In one hand, a Popsicle in the other.
Nice dog, I said, while Humo sniffed
The lawn, his nose wet
And black as tar. The girl was drawing

A face on the sidewalk,
Face of someone not unlike herself, troubled,
For the mouth was slanted evilly.
He's a nice doggie, I repeated,
This time in Spanish. Would you like a dog?
The girl gazed up and brought out a tongue,
Red as the devil's pitchfork.
Ay, Dios, I screamed and rose to my feet,
Scared: No telling who might
Later say, Yes, he was the man!
Yes, he was the one who touched her,
You know, down there. I hurried
Off to the courthouse park,
Humo running in and out of shadow.
The leaves of the tall sycamore
Slit the breeze, and some of its coolness
Went to the children on the swings,
Some to *viejos* like myself.
On the bench I listened to something
About *la chupacabra*, the monster
Who sucks blood from goats,
And shook my head.
These old men bleated out stories,
Some gripping canes, their sweaters
Buttoned all wrong, the shrubbery
Of hair hanging from their ears.
I murmured, Am I as old as them?
I thought of rocks, rivers brown
From crumbling banks,
Bird nests abandoned in the bare trees.
I asked, Am I this old? I touched my ears,
My own shrubbery hanging from the holes.
I got up, stiffly, my steps at first the steps
Of a spider. I threw a stick, and the dog fetched.
I threw it a second time,
A third, and finally hurled it with

All my strength, then hurried away,
Almost running, in the direction
Of a church with a roof
Pitched so steeply that sinners
Would slide down and smack concrete—
I considered a spot on the cement.
Yes, this is where I will fall, please, God.
I don't want no more.
I looked around: The dog was gone,
A stick in its mouth, tail perhaps wagging,
The dog mustering up his dog thoughts.
My own mind whirled. I entered
The church and sat near the altar.
The dog is gone, I told myself,
And suddenly I was on my knees,
Hands laced, and praying *for* my hands and knees,
My two body parts that pained me in winter.
Was I asking much? I closed my eyes, opened them.
I noticed my knuckles like the exposed rings
Of a chopped-down tree.
My feet hurt, a bone in the small of my back clicked,
And sweat washed my chest
And belly, two fallen empires.
I prayed deep as the roots of an ancient tree.
When I opened my eyes,
Humo was near the baptismal font,
Lapping splashed water at the marble base.
Ay, Dios, I cried, and Humo picked up
His stick and came running.

*

Wind knocked at the screen door,
Wind rapped the anemic arms
Of ivy against the window.
Or so I thought as I struggled from the couch,

An effort itself because I was sunken
In its worn springs. Who's there? I asked.
It's me, Blanca, my neighbor announced
Thickly through the heavy door.
When I opened up, she rushed in
With a small suitcase.
I asked, Where are you going, *vieja*?
I imagined the contents of the case—
A brood of chickens, the rooster and hen,
And—God help me—a pair of her underwear,
The pink ones I had seen repeatedly
Swinging on the clothesline.
Hombre, what are you doing with
A spoon in your hand? Blanca asked.
I looked down at my hand
And, yes, there was a soup spoon
And a stain on the front of my shirt,
The stain of old age from a quivering hand?
Blanca bellowed, *¡Ayúdame, hombre!*
As I followed her to the kitchen.
Humo barked on the steps,
Pressed his nose to the screen door,
Whined, this dog that wouldn't go away.
Blanca, how can I help? I asked,
The soup spoon now in the sink
And me pulling at my sweater,
Trying my best to hide the stain
On my shirt. Did I have to replace
A lightbulb, perhaps waltz
A piece of heavy furniture across
Her living room and into a bedroom?
Or maybe she wanted me to take a hatchet
To the rooster. Blanca hoisted
A sly smile, and spilled lipstick, eyeliner,
And bottles of cologne on the table, a treasure.
She had taken a job selling cosmetics,

Door to door if need be, and wanted
Me—good God—to play the female client,
Me with the complexion of a potato.
Mujer, I cried and nearly grabbed
The spoon in the kitchen sink
And returned to my bowl to slurp my broth.
But she pressed against me,
A woman with the scent of everything
She carried in the suitcase—
Lavender and lemon came to mind.
You can, she cooed, and suddenly
I was playing along, a client,
And asking, *¿Cuanto? How much?*
I was holding up a bottle of cologne,
And Blanca was scolding playfully, *No, hombre.*
Estás hablando como un bruto.
She reminded me that I was playing
A woman, though of course
She knew I was a man, what with my underwear
On the clothesline, the soup stain
On my shirt, the nests of
Hair in my nostrils. She smiled
And said: Let's try again. I narrowed my eyes
At the lipstick—"Mango Madness"
Another labeled "Suddenly Shocking"
Oh, gee whiz, I said in a high voice,
Oh, how pretty! Blanca laughed
And spanked her lap, her dress
Pressed between her thighs. She shoved eyeliner
Into my hands, a thin chrome cylinder
I turned in my hands. The eyeliner
Was called "Hawaiian Reef,"
And I didn't know
What to say except, How much for three dollars?
Her laughter started Humo barking.
She gathered the treasure back

Into her suitcase. *Hombre,*
You are a bad client, she said,
And gazed at the stove
With its industry of buckled and blackened pots.
She sniffed the air. Let's have soup!
She cried. What could I do but get up
And walk six steps to the stove?
When she was gone, I noticed the smudge
Of Mango Madness on the lip of a large mug.

*

I pulled the larger dog off Humo
And screamed, You think this is funny?
The three *cholos* laughed,
Glue rags in their limp hands.
One said, Old man, kill yourself.
If younger, I would have grabbed his throat
And pulled out the windpipe embedded there,
Let him slither like a snake.
If stronger, I could have sunk a fist
Into that soft stomach.
Those idiot boys had been talking
About the placement of speakers
In their cars, one asking, Shit, man,
Why put speakers near your feet
When your ears are in your head?
Tu sabes, you know what I mean, bro?
I hadn't looked at them.
Trouble is what they were.
But they called their dog on Humo,
Who raised his eyes up at me for help,
Poor dog of mine who lives
On the scraps of an old man
And now this? The *cholo* dog
Made a lot of noise around Humo's throat,

The two dogs flipping wildly on the sidewalk
And me screaming, ¡Para! ¡Para!
The *cholos* held me back,
Laughing and saying, This is a good one.
When Humo was free, the two of us hurried away.

In the courthouse park
I searched Humo's throat for wounds,
Two small ones, both bloodless.
I patted them with spit,
And was peeling crust from his eyes
When I heard a bark. I feared the other dog was back,
The mean one with fur in his mouth.
Then I saw: The commotion
Of *la migra,* the border patrol,
They themselves far from the border
And now chasing men across the park.
Everyone became still,
The children on the swings,
The mothers working the tops
Off baby bottles, a man stomping
Soda cans near the dumpster.
Humo moved under the bench,
And I stood up, whispered,
This is the courthouse park, my God.
I imagined the robed judges
Inside in the cold halls, their hair white
From having to hear so much,
None of the judges asking,
Why in the world are car speakers
Placed near our feet? No,
The judges were hearing about human slaughter,
And we out in the courthouse park
Were watching men,
None of them too fast,
All of them with the telltale sign

Of immigrants—gold teeth.
Only after *la migra* was gone,
Did the babies begin to cry
And the mothers fit the bottles
In their mouths to stop it all.

*

Blanca said, No, move to the left,
And I sidled to my left,
The rosebush grabbing my sweater,
Rosebush with its dead crowns,
With its red laughter of petals all dried up.
I unhooked my sweater, knelt slowly,
For the hinges in my knees
Were worn, for my head was large,
My belly, my chest with its saddles of fat.
I petted Humo and said, It's for us,
As Blanca aimed an unsteady camera.
Later I saw that my head
Was gone, chopped off.
I saw that Humo, a blur,
Was biting my shoelaces.
She snapped the camera two more times,
And I was gone with Humo
At my side, the wag of happiness
In his tail. We walked over
To the unemployment office,
Where men and women were hustling
Through the doors. The security guard,
A Filipino with watery eyes,
Sniffed at Humo and didn't say anything
Like, No dogs here. No, no!
He let us pass, this mule of a man
Who stood at the glass door
Smudged with the fingers of the unemployed,

The unemployable. I took my place
At a board of job listings.
I saw farmworkers were needed,
A gardener, a delivery person,
Something about telemarketing.
Three men gawked at the board,
Mouths open, the wind of boredom
Drying their tongues. I said
To myself, I can drive a bakery truck,
And pictured myself with a donut
Clamped in my jaws
As I struggled with the steering wheel,
Me the captain of sweets.
I said, Yes, I can rake leaves,
And, yes, I can pick up a telephone
And shout, Sir, you are a winner!
But I realized that at sixty-five, a borderline diabetic,
I couldn't spin a donut on my thumb
And chew for my pleasure.
I was an old man who would add
The grease of his own fingerprints
To the glass door when he left.
Why not, I said, feel sorry for yourself,
Blow your nose in the handkerchief of defeat.
Then I looked down. Humo, the rascal,
Had nibbled the shoelaces of the three men,
All of them absorbed in finding work.
A comedy was occurring right at their feet.

*

Did the hen cry under a knife?
Did the rooster struggle from the hatchet?
Blanca screamed, *Gané, hombre*. I won!
As I was leaving my apartment
To—what was it again?—to buy

A can of soup, day-old bread,
Bruised fruit from the farmers' market
Mujer, I said, you are lucky.
She ignored me. She touched
My sleeve and said, You smell good.
I thought, Yes, that's true.
And almost said: Blanca,
I'm sixty-five, dead down below,
But what man wants to admit this
On a fall day when his appetite
Is for an apple peeled by a pocketknife.
I wanted to step back into my apartment,
But the door was closed, the keys
Heavy in my pocket. I sighed
And examined the lottery ticket,
Then heard something like wind.
Blanca and I raised our faces skyward—
A blimp with no signs like Goodyear or Fuji Film.
This one was silver, nearly invisible,
Except to old people like Blanca and me.
Those studying signs of departure.
I shaded my eyes and thought,
My son died looking at a blimp.
If he had lived, he would have been thirty-one,
But what is put in the earth stays in the earth.
But I know this: the earth speaks
To us through trees and rivers,
The rumbles of small quakes.
But the dead, *pues*, their jaws are locked
And their mouths heavy with rocks.
Then Blanca pulled my shirtsleeve.
You got to buy a ticket, she said,
So I said, What is my lucky number?
Blanca answered, It's whatever age
You are. *Ay, Dios,* I sighed,
And left walking up the street,

My dog, Humo, running in and
Out of my shadow, oh, my poor
Crippled shadow the color
Of ash, shadow that was lines
On the sidewalk. I wanted to hold my head
And tell it, Head, you'll be OK.
I thought, I must think about my food,
What is it—a can of soup?
Instant coffee? Eggs? No, no,
It must be a bag of oranges. Then I heard
The blimp but didn't look up
As its darkness swooped at
My shadow, Humo's shadow.
I saw who I was, ash blowing on the road,
And grew angry at that blimp,
A mechanical god who took my son
Thirteen years ago. *Cabrón*, I yelled,
And began running in the direction of the blimp,
A mistake of the heart. I was running
After my death, I told myself,
And taking with me this dog, Humo,
Dog who sometimes ran up front,
Then behind, but mostly, how strange,
He ran at my side with one eye on me.
The blimp rode between the clouds,
Blimp the size of God's fist. I slowed
To a walk. The dog trotted ahead
In pursuit of something I couldn't touch—
Love I believe, the past I am certain,
A son's hand in mine and a flurry
Of autumn leaves fluttering back into the trees.

Photo: Carolyn Soto

Gary Soto is a poet, playwright, essayist, and author of several children's books. Widely anthologized, he is a frequent contributor to such magazines as *The Threepenny Review, Michigan Quarterly, Crazy Horse,* and *Poetry,* which has honored him with both the Bess Hokin and Levinson Prizes. He has received the Discovery–The Nation Award, as well as the Andrew Carnegie Medal for Film Excellence, the Literature Award from the Hispanic Heritage Award Foundation, and an American Book Award from the Before Columbus Foundation. He has also received fellowships from the Guggenheim Foundation, the National Endowment for the Arts, and the California Arts Council. A National Book Award Finalist for *New and Selected Poems* (Chronicle Books), Gary Soto divides his time between Berkeley and his hometown of Fresno.